# Debt Management

*A Guide To Getting (And Staying) Out of Debt*

RON KNESS

No part of this book may be reproduced, stored in a retrieval system, or transmitted in any form or by any means, electronic, mechanical, photocopying, recording, scanning, or otherwise, without the prior written permission of the publisher, except for the inclusion of brief quotations in a review.
This book is for **personal use only**.

Copyright © 2017 Ron Kness
All rights reserved.
**ISBN-13: 978-1546326694**
**ISBN-10: 1546326693**

# Contents

Disclaimer ............................................................................ 1

Introduction – DEBT: A Four Letter Word That Could Ruin Your Life ............................................................................ 2

Good Debt and Bad Debt – Know the Difference ................... 4

Are You in a Debt Spiral? ....................................................... 8

Those Nagging Student Loans – What are Your Options? ...10

First Step for Getting Out of Debt – Develop a Budget ........ 13

Negotiating for Tax Relief ..................................................... 16

Pros and Cons of Using a Debt Consolidation Service ........ 19

How to Deal with Debt Collectors ......................................... 21

Protecting Your Funds from Debt Garnishment .................. 24

Have a Get Out of Debt Emergency Plan ............................. 29

Using a Home Equity Loan or Refinance Option to Get Out of Debt .................................................................................. 31

Steps to Getting Out of Debt Forever ................................... 34

Borrowing from Friends or Family ....................................... 36

Credit Counseling Agencies – Do They Really Help? .......... 39

Steps to Financial Freedom ........................................................ 45

Final Thoughts - Life After Debt .............................................. 47

Monthly Sample Budget ............................................................ 49

About the Author ........................................................................ 50

# Disclaimer

This publication is for informational purposes only and is not intended as financial advice. Matters involving money, credit and debt should always be obtained from a qualified finance professional.

Every possible effort has been made in preparing and researching this material. However, we make no warranties with respect to the accuracy, applicability of its contents or any omissions.

**See your finance professional before starting any debt management or credit repair program!**

# Introduction – DEBT: A Four Letter Word That Could Ruin Your Life

We all know that too much of a good thing isn't good for you. Too much debt isn't good for you either – but neither is too little debt.

When you're in debt to the point that you can't make payments on time and your credit score tanks, it can make your life miserable.

Some necessities, such as a home in which to live or a car to drive to work and back, may not be available if your credit score is low; if you do qualify for either, you may end up paying a higher interest rate because of your lower credit score. And if you have no credit at all, these things could also be beyond your grasp.

The best path to follow when it comes to debt is to build your credit so your score is high, but always have the ability to pay cash for anything you might purchase – except for high-dollar items such as a house or car.

Creditors look at credit card debt as bad debt because you're only required to make a minimum monthly payment on what you owe. You can keep using your card until the balance is maxed out and that looks bad on your credit report.

Think again if you consider credit card debt as good debt because you don't have to pay for your purchases right away.

You could end up spending more than you have the ability to pay back as interest charges are incurred and you get in trouble fast.

When you begin to have trouble paying your bills, you'll also begin to get notices from creditors for the balances you owe or they might be turned over to debt collectors. You may even become rightly concerned about losing your house or car if you can't make the payments on time and penalties and interest keep climbing.

Losing your job or meeting a financial crisis such as health problems can turn your financial situation upside down and you may find it an overwhelming task to dig your way out.

Rather than ignoring your situation and letting the debt problems become worse, take steps to get yourself out of the mess by being realistic. Help yourself by cutting unnecessary spending, creating a budget and sticking to it. You may also want to consider debt consolidation or debt relief such as debt settlement or credit counseling.

Bankruptcy may become an option when you've tried everything else, but still are mired in debt. If you're experiencing a level of debt and other problems such as loss of a job or medical situation which requires immediate payment, bankruptcy may be the best option.

When you are finally free of debt, it's time to rebuild your credit. For this, you have to have discipline and never again let yourself be swayed by credit card and loan offers that will simply put you back in debt and keep your life in chaos.

These are all topics we discuss in this guide. Let's get started ....

# Good Debt and Bad Debt – Know the Difference

Non-consumer loans are classified as good debt and consumer loans are considered to be bad debt. Basically, non-consumer loans fall into the category of offering low interest rates, collateral that will likely increase in value and tax advantages.

Consumer loans are viewed as bad debt because of their high interest rates, no collateral that can be used to secure a loan and no tax advantages. You should know the difference in these two types of debts before attempting to secure a loan and be able to determine which is to your best advantage.

A lender will look closely at your credit card debt and see if you either pay balances every month or pay a minimum payment that incurs high interest charges. Credit cards also offer no advantages such as tax advantages and you're only required to pay a small percentage of your balance to keep using your card (until you max out your credit limit).

Credit cards can become an Achilles' heel fast and cause you to mire deeper and deeper into debt. Having the ability to spend without paying for something right away is tempting, but can cause each and every item you purchase with a credit card to cost infinitely more than the sticker cost.

However today, it's almost impossible to live completely debt free. Few people have the money on hand to pay entirely for such purchases as a car, home or private education. That's why it's so important that you know the difference between good and bad debt and apply for loans accordingly.

Good debts should be considered an investment that will likely appreciate in value or provide income. Although student loans have gotten a bad rap, they're considered good debt because a college education boosts your chances of raising your future income.

Another way to think of consumer debt is that it's held by individuals rather than the government. Household debt is also considered consumer debt and statistically the debt service ratio (DSR) that calculates each household's debt compared to the total income of the household.

DSR doesn't include rent or mortgage payments. These payments are calculated with a financial obligations ratio (FOR). Today, most homeowners spend up to 20% of their household income on the mortgage payment.

It's important to know exactly how much your bad debt totals and pay off these debts as soon as possible. The best way to do that is to formulate a budget and curb your spending habits until you save enough cash to pay off the bad debts.

Your budget should include how much you intend to spend for food, mortgage (or rental) payments and clothing, savings and entertainment. Adhering to a well-thought-out budget plan will help you lower your overall debt.

## The Difference Between Consumer and Non-Consumer Debts

It's imperative that you know the difference between consumer and non-consumer debts and how each may affect your credit and your lifestyle. The difference in the two types of debts lies in the manner they're treated when it comes to taxes, annual percentage rates, terms of agreement and collateral you may offer.

A non-consumer debt is usually covered by an asset which is expected to appreciate in value, such as a home. The asset acts as collateral for the loan you receive from a lending institution, meaning if you don't pay back the loan, the lender can sell the property and retain the money received.

APRs (annual percentage rate) are usually much less for non-consumer debts because they're less risky for the lender. APRs usually coincide with the risk the lender is taking if you fail to pay back the loan and if there is collateral for the loan amount, the risk is minimal.

Interest on most non-consumer debts are usually completely tax deductible and you can take off the amount from your taxes owed each year. Also, most non-consumer debts usually offer a fixed term agreement on the loan, meaning that you have a set time to pay off the debt and can plan better for this fixed amount and timeline.

Consumer debts are usually considered bad debt because you're purchasing items based on no collateral and can keep adding to the debt and paying the accrued interest.

Credit cards are the most common type of consumer debt, but auto loans or other major purchases are also considered loans for general purposes.

The interest on consumer loans is usually not tax deductible and can run up your debts to exorbitant amounts in a hurry because of high interest rates. Sometimes the rates change and can run as high as 30%.

Consumer debts usually have no set time to pay off the amount owed and this is a great situation for the lenders because the rates ensure that you're paying off the purchases for years and paying them extra in the form of interest in the meantime.

Credit card consumer debt is dangerous to the borrower because it's not fully understood. Remember that you're only required to make a minimum payment on your balance (perhaps 2 or 3 percent).

If you have a $1,000 balance on a card at the end of the month, you may only have to pay $10 or $15 in payment. In fact, the interest on those purchases might exceed your payment amount. Make an effort to pay off credit card balances each month to avoid paying high interest rates. Never charge more than you can pay with cash if needed.

# Are You in a Debt Spiral?

A debt spiral is pretty much like a bad nightmare where you're falling into nothingness and can't get yourself out of it. Many people go through debt spirals in their lifetime because of unforeseen expenses, loss of a job or medical crisis.

Sometimes it's by no fault of your own that the debt spiral occurs, and other times it's because spending habits were out of control. Whatever the reason you find yourself in a debt spiral, it's time to spend less, make more money – or both.

It may take a while to unravel the tangled mess you find yourself in, but you're sure to learn more about how to better manage your money and a little bit about yourself, too. The first thing to do if you find yourself deep in debt is to assess your damage.

How much do you owe, to whom do you owe it and what interest rates are you paying? You should assess everything in your litany of debts, but especially focus on consumer debts such as credit cards.

Find the root cause of your financial problems. That can only be done by tracking your spending. You'll then begin to understand the weak spots of your spending habits and be able to focus on areas where you can cut back.

Most debit and credit card expenditures are easy to track – or you can do it the old way, by saving and adding up receipts. After you know where your money is going you can include the entire family in your plan to cut back.

Don't cut out everything that the family enjoys, but do include them in the effort to trim some of the fat from your spending habits. If you need more help than a budget plan to cut back on expenses, consider a consolidation loan to reduce your multiple payments to one and to stop the high interest rate you may be experiencing on credit cards.

Being unable to make payments to creditors on time can ruin your credit standing and even lead to harsher measures such as bankruptcy. One signal that you're in a debt spiral is that you can't afford to pay your credit cards in full each month.

You keep using your credit cards to purchase necessities such as food and medicine and the creditors add an exorbitant amount of interest to the balance each month. You may even borrow to pay bills – a sure sign you need to sit down and carefully assess your spending and what got you in this predicament in the first place.

Don't assume that the road will be smooth after you get yourself out of the debt spiral. You have to get to the root of your spending problem and take steps to keep you from ever having this problem again.

# Those Nagging Student Loans – What are Your Options?

It's always best to know your options when addressing any debt. Student loans can especially be a long and complicated process that might seem overwhelming and even put your good credit at risk if you don't pay on time.

There's a lot at stake, so you should know how to manage student loan debt. One thing you need to know before acquiring a student loan is to first look for federal student loans.

Private loans aren't backed by the federal government and you can pay more interest – plus, they're risky to your ongoing credit. When you're ready, fill out the free FAFSA application – **F**ree **A**pplication for **F**ederal **S**tudent **A**id. Their website is at: https://fafsa.ed.gov/.

If you decide to take out a federal student aid loan, you'll be paying back the loan with interest, but the interest rate will be lower and the payment options will be more flexible. The amount of the loan you can secure depends on whether you are an undergraduate or graduate student.

Parents of undergraduate students can also apply for a federal student loan for costs not covered in other types of financial aid. A credit check is usually required for a parent (PLUS) loan.

# DEBT MANAGEMENT

After you secure a loan, make sure you keep in touch with your loan servicer (bank or government). Managing your student loan properly is the best way to stay out of financial difficulties and know your options before problems occur.

Make sure you update loan servicers with new information about your whereabouts, such as new address, phone number and email address. That will also ensure that you'll be updated about the servicer's important communications to you.

Contact your lender immediately if you're having trouble making payments on time. If you've secured a federal loan, you might be able to temporarily suspend or reduce your payments.

Ignoring the late payment consequences might include ruining your credit score, increasing the amount you must pay or garnishment of any wages you might earn. Finding yourself drowning in debt from student loans and other life circumstances can be devastating.

There is a program called "Public Service Loan Forgiveness" which may forgive a debt after 10 years of repayment. The qualifications include that you currently work for the government or a nonprofit agency or certain other public service jobs.

You may also qualify if you're a teacher, medical personnel or are serving in the military. The good news is that a four-year college graduate is much better able to find employment and earn a higher salary than those who only graduate high school.

Getting an education can be very expensive and grants and scholarships have been reduced and have failed to rise as fast as tuitions. Avoid misunderstandings of student loan repayments by keeping in touch with your lender and making sure you understand your options before signing on the dotted line.

# First Step for Getting Out of Debt – Develop a Budget

The first and most important step for getting – and staying – out of debt is to create a workable budget. Whether you use a spreadsheet or other form of tracking your spending, you'll feel more empowered when it comes to your finances and can finally begin to save money for things you want and need when you know exactly where your money is going.

First, assess your net income – the money you bring home for expenses. Make sure you don't use your total salary as your net income, but only what you get to spend after taxes and other deductions.

Your final take-home pay is the net income you'll use when creating a workable budget. Next, track every penny of your spending for a month. This will be able to help you make adjustments in the way you spend money and identify where the problem areas are.

Some people are surprised where their money is going when they take a hard look at it. Set reachable goals – those that you want to accomplish that are both short and long term.

When you set short term goals, have in mind a year or less to get them paid. Long term goals may take years to accomplish. You can change your goals from time to time, but make sure you stick to a general plan of action.

You'll want to know what your variable and fixed expenses are so you can accurately predict the amounts in your budget. Check out your past records for spending to predict your variable expenses.

The variable and fixed expense reports will give you a good idea of what you'll be spending during the year ahead. Fixed expenses will likely be more accurate than variable ones such as clothing and unexpected medical expenses.

Take a hard look at the habits you've developed in the past and adjust them so that you're not leaching money that could be used to pay off bills or other needed or wanted goals.

Look for cuts you can make to your spending and try adjusting the numbers in your budget so you can eventually accomplish your goals. Don't work on a budget and then forget about it.

That's the surest way to go back to your old spending habits. By keeping an itemized budget, you can easily look back to see how you've spent each dollar and adjust as you move on and pay off nagging bills.

Make sure you know your goals and consult your plans periodically as you would a map on a cross-country trip. One mistake many people make when formulating a budget is to cut out all of the fun in their lives.

But rather than cut out all restaurant meals, simply cut down on how many times you eat out as a family. Rather than taking your lunch to work every day, allocate one day a week to go out with friends. You are in control of your finances – make your money work for you.

# Negotiating for Tax Relief

Receiving a letter or other type of contact with the Internal Revenue Service can be scary and intimidating – especially if you don't know or understand your options. Never ignore the problem, but meet it head-on.

Hoping it will just go away isn't an option. Written correspondence from the IRS is a red flag that you should take immediate action. That may mean that you can try to negotiate with them for some type of tax relief.

Always respond as soon as possible to any communications you get from the IRS and answer all questions related to the matter. Talking to them by phone on a one-on-one basis is often a better option than snail mail.

Make sure you document who you're talking to and any resolution that was reached during the call. Your best chance for successful negotiation with the IRS is to file your taxes on time.

This reduces your chances of incurring any penalties. It also helps you negotiate a settlement which might be less than what you owe (based on what you can afford) or entering into an installment agreement which lets you pay in monthly installments.

Rather than feeling intimidated, take immediate control of your tax situation. Never ignore the problem. Although negotiating with the IRS may cause stress, it's usually best to deal with the IRS on a personal level rather than hiring a tax relief company.

If you absolutely don't understand or don't have the capacity to deal with the IRS, there are legitimate tax relief organizations that can help you get through the maze by helping to negotiate the installment agreement, reduce penalties and keep your wages from being garnished.

Some IRS settlement options that you may not be aware of include a partial payment installment agreement which lets you use a long-term payment plan and a reduced dollar amount to pay your debt in installments rather than all at once.

Another method is called "Offer in Compromise," which lets you settle your tax debts for a lesser amount than what you currently owe. You may be required to pay a lump sum or use a short-term payment plan, but if you owe more than you can pay, this may be the best option to negotiate.

The program, "Not Currently Collectible" means that the IRS agrees to let your tax debt ride for a year or so. This may be a good method if you have no way to pay back the tax debt – and, you can file an appeal to halt seizures, an IRS levy or liens on your property.

There are no secret methods to negotiating tax relief, but there are ways to stop the IRS' debt collection methods which can be aggressive at times.

Keep in mind that the IRS does have the power to seize your assets, garnish wages or place a lien on any property you might own to get the money you owe.

You can prevent these actions by proper communication with the IRS. They're usually amenable to working with honest taxpayers who reach out to them to help resolve your debt problems.

# Pros and Cons of Using a Debt Consolidation Service

Debt consolidation services can be a big help to getting out of debt and staying out of debt. Secured consolidation loans are secured with collateral, which means it's less risk for the lender. Unsecured consolidation loans use none of your collateral, but may charge a higher APR.

Either way, you'll benefit from consolidating all your loans into one monthly payment with one lower APR. Secured loans will provide the lowest APR and they're the easier of the two to obtain.

If you decide to use home equity to secure a consolidation loan, you'll also have the advantage of being able to deduct the interest on your tax return. Unless you own a home, car or other assets such as land or a boat, you can't apply for a secured consolidation loan.

The amount of the collateral you're securing must be at least enough to cover the loan amount. Keep in mind that with a secured loan, the lender can seize your asset if you are found in default of the loan.

Unsecured consolidation loans don't require collateral to secure the loan, so you might end up with a higher APR. It's still a good way to go because you're likely to have a lower APR than most of the debts you're consolidating.

It's not a good idea to get an unsecured loan through a credit card. These offers involve combining all your current credit card balances into one, new credit card which has a lower APR. This may sound like a good idea, but it's not the best route to take for several reasons.

One reason is that the new, low APR is only temporary. After a few months, the rate changes to a higher rate. Most credit card companies who offer consolidation of loans also tack on a fee (can range from $50 to $100) for each balance you transfer from other credit cards. This can add up in a hurry.

You may also incur a lower credit score when you open a new credit card account – especially if you max it out right away. Consolidating your debts by credit card may also mean that you stay in debt for a long period of time, since most companies don't set a certain time limit for you to pay it off.

Check with your bank and several others before applying for a consolidation loan to see which can offer the best rate. If you belong to a credit union, you may get the lowest APR rate possible. Credit unions are non-profit, but restrictions for membership are often stringent.

# How to Deal with Debt Collectors

Those harassed by debt collectors often panic from the pestering. Constant phone calls, being abusive on the phone, calling at work or late at night are not acceptable and should not be tolerated.

If you have an outstanding bill and are being harassed by debt collectors, you should know your rights. For example, ask for a written notice stating how much you owe, who the creditor is and your rights from the debt collection act if you believe you don't owe the demanded money.

You should receive a written notice within five days. Challenge the debt in writing within thirty days of the written notice if you don't believe you owe the amount (or owe nothing) demanded from you.

Make sure you keep all written communication between you and the creditor or debt collector. Send your response letter by certified mail and keep all receipts so you can prove you responded properly and within the allotted time.

And of course, keep all records of phone calls, messages and other types of communications between you and the debt collector. Keep a log of the day and time called and a brief summary about what was discussed.

Also, make sure you get the debt collector's name and agency name and the amount they say you owe. Keep any voice mail the collector may leave.

There are particular rules that debt collectors must follow such as harassment with many calls, abusive language, calling before 8 A.M. in the morning or after 9 P.M. in the evening unless you told them to call at that time.

If they call you at work, you can ask them to stop and they have to adhere to your wishes. They can't disclose your information to anyone else other than you or your attorney.

They can't claim to be law enforcement or a lawyer or a representative from a credit bureau. The representative from the debt collection agency can't threaten you by saying they're going to sue, seize your property or garnish your wages unless they've taken appropriate action to do it and can prove it to you.

Legitimate debt collectors will usually be willing to negotiate, and if you know you owe the money, you may be able to work out a deal that's less than the amount they're demanding.

Offer ten or fifteen percent of the amount you owe and be prepared to settle for about half of the actual amount.

The debt collector may be able to remove the debt from your credit report, so push for that in any negotiations you agree to. Before you pay the agreed amount, get the details of the negotiation in writing. Never give your account number or other information to the collector – and make sure you pay with a cashier's check rather than a personal check.

# Protecting Your Funds from Debt Garnishment

If you're in debt to the point that creditors are calling and threatening to garnish your wages or other funds, you should know what your options are to keep creditors at bay until you can straighten out your financial situation.

Perhaps one of your creditors obtained a judgment from you many years ago and you've since forgotten about it. You may think the creditor simply wrote it off as a bad debt.

Then you get a letter of Complaint to Enforce Judgment and an application to apply for garnishment of your bank accounts and wages. You do have some options if this happens to you.

You can challenge the judgment for its validity or claim exemption or hardship. If you believe a judgment was wrongfully executed and taken against you, you can challenge it in a court of law.

Usually, the judgement is obtained lawfully and you do owe the debt. If that's the case, some states will let you place a motion to halt or limit the seizure of wages or funds based on hardship.

Some states let you file an exemption because you qualify as head of household. Make sure you research your states exemption laws to see about other exemptions such as Social Security, Worker's Compensation, Unemployment Insurance, retirement and pension benefits, VA benefits and SSI benefits to see if you may qualify.

Bankruptcy is another way to protect your assets from garnishment. If you're deep in debt and qualify for bankruptcy, all legal action that could be taken against you are immediately frozen the moment you file.

The good thing about bankruptcy is that your wages can't be garnished and your home or car can't be repossessed. Chapters 7, 11 or 13 are all types of bankruptcy that will block garnishment.

The debt involved is either erased from your debts owed or a trustee will help you with a payment plan later when you have reorganized your assets and are able to pay it back. You should also look carefully at the bank accounts you currently have open and plan how to handle it so your creditor doesn't have the account number or even the name of the bank unless the court orders you to do so.

You may be tempted to withdraw the cash from all your bank accounts immediately, but consider first using such cash cards as PayPal to draw your money from. Put a hold on all direct deposits that might be sent, since those can be immediately garnished.

Make sure you stay within the law when attempting to protect your funds from garnishment. If you have to submit to an Order of Examination from the court, you'll likely have to release the name of your employer and give an accounting of your assets.

## When to File Bankruptcy

Bankruptcy should be the last resort to fixing your credit problems. You should know what your options are before you make the decision to file. Filing for bankruptcy is a serious decision that you should think long and hard about.

Most of your debts can be removed from your credit record by filing for bankruptcy, but it can also have serious consequences. A bankruptcy will show on your credit reports for 10 years - and meantime, you'll be unable to secure a loan except at a very high interest rate.

You should decide to file for bankruptcy only if you've exhausted other avenues for help and you are in a financial emergency. Those with consumer debts usually file a Chapter 7 type of bankruptcy, where the court issues an automatic stay which keeps creditors from contacting you during the bankruptcy procedures.

This liquidation type of bankruptcy requires that you present detailed reports about all of your assets, income, expenses and outstanding debts. A discharge of all debts usually occurs after three to six months and costs around $300 to file.

If you hire an attorney to help you through the paperwork maze, you'll pay more. Even though a bankruptcy judgment will stay on your credit record for years, the decision is better than hurting your credit with missed payments, repossessions, defaults and lawsuits.

Bankruptcy is often easier to explain to a lender than having to explain each debt you defaulted on. Many things you own such as car, home and furniture will be exempt from bankruptcy procedures and anything you purchase after the bankruptcy is also free from seizure.

Your wages or salary is exempt, too. You'll lose all of your credit cards (consumer debt) and you won't likely be able to secure another mortgage. Lenders often consider bankruptcy customers as high risk, but you may be able to secure possessions after bankruptcy at much higher interest rates.

If you find yourself deep in debt again shortly after filing Chapter 7 bankruptcy, you might be able to file for Chapter 13 bankruptcy. Keep in mind, every filing of bankruptcy appears on your credit record and makes it more difficult for you to purchase things in the future.

Deciding to file bankruptcy is a major decision in your life. It will affect your future credit and lifestyle plans, self-esteem and your reputation.

But it can also relieve the stress and angst that being deep in debt with no way out can bring to your life.

A local attorney can provide you with an initial claim review to discuss your situation and counsel you on the law involved in filing bankruptcy. This review is free and can help you make this monumental decision.

# Have a Get Out of Debt Emergency Plan

Heavy debt can make you feel as if you're drowning. You may feel like an elephant is sitting on your chest preventing you from breathing, feel out of control and feel panic that keeps you from thinking clearly.

Until you formulate a plan for getting out of debt, you'll keep floundering and the debt situation will only get worse. When you're finally determined to rectify the situation by doing everything possible to get out of debt – it's time to formulate a plan.

First, carefully assess your debts. You can request a free credit report each year from the three credit bureaus – TransUnion, Equifax and Experian. You'll likely find that you're even more in debt than you realize.

After you carefully analyze your situation, you can take a plan of action. If you've had some especially bad marks on your credit reports – such as charge offs – you may be able to negotiate with the creditor(s) or work with a debt counseling service.

Most people hate the word, "budget," but that's the next step in ensuring you get out of debt as soon as possible. Alter your lifestyle to exclude everything you're spending money on that isn't necessary.

Take your lunch rather than buying it every day, slash your cable and Internet services to the minimum, check car and other insurance programs to see if you can adjust your deductibles and lower your premiums, walk rather than working out at a gym and look at other monthly spending to see where you can cut out or lower payments and spending.

After you've tweaked your budget all you can, you likely have some extra money to pay on bills. If it's not enough to stretch as far as it takes to pay all your bills, contact some of the businesses where you've accrued small bills to see if you can work out a plan.

Try to pay the bills which are regularly reported to credit bureaus. Make sure you pay your rent or mortgage first and then pay on the loans or credit cards which have the highest interest rates. Then pay the as much as possible on the remainder of your debts.

Stabilize your credit by doing things that will restore your credit score with credit bureaus. Establish a savings account with your bank and perhaps get a prepaid credit card.

These steps will show creditors that you're serious about reestablishing your good credit and that you're taking the necessary steps to repay your debts. Realize that you do have options and that filing for bankruptcy should be the last one you consider.

DEBT MANAGEMENT

# Using a Home Equity Loan or Refinance Option to Get Out of Debt

Homeowners can take advantage of a home equity loan or refinance option to get out of a debt spiral by using the money to consolidate consumer debts. Using a home equity loan means that you take out money against the equity you've paid into your home based on the difference between the amount you  owe on the mortgage and the current value of the home.

For example, if you currently owe $200,000 on a home worth $300,000 at current market value, you're eligible for $100,000 home equity loan. The two types of home equity loans include securing a second mortgage or getting a home equity line of credit.

The second mortgage means that you get a loan equal to or a portion of the equity you currently have in your home. You'll continue paying the original mortgage payment, plus an additional monthly payment (plus interest) to pay back the home equity loan.

You can use the money from the loan to pay down your existing consumer debts – or for any other purpose. The money is yours to use however you see fit and the good news is that the interest on the second mortgage is normally 100% tax deductible up to $100,000.

Getting a home equity line of credit is also an option for using some fast money to pay down your consumer debts. A HELOC lets you borrow against the amount of equity you have in your home in increments rather than borrowing a set amount all at once.

It may not be the best option if you have a great amount of debt to pay. Refinancing your home (cash-out refinancing) is also an option when you need money to pay off nagging consumer debts.

Know that the new mortgage amount will exceed the balance on your current mortgage so that you can use the extra amount for paying off your debts and the main amount to pay off the old mortgage.

You'll usually get a good rate for cash-out refinancing, but the deal is only available to those debtors who currently have a mortgage they're paying off. If you have to choose between a cash-out refinancing option or a second mortgage (home equity loan), the second mortgage may be the best option if you have enough equity in your home to cover the debts you've incurred.

Remember that you're responsible for both the second mortgage and the cash-out refinancing options. Use the money for how it is intended – to pay off consumer debts and get out of a debt spiral or you may find yourself in the same, or worse, predicament.

# Steps to Getting Out of Debt Forever

Many of us live in the moment when it comes to finances – if the money is there, or the credit is available, spend it or take advantage of it. If you truly want to get out of debt and remain out of debt, there are some steps you can take to make sure you avoid getting back in to the same old rut while you're paying off present debt.

Always remember that when you put that great sale item you found on a credit card, you're paying much more than it initially cost. Credit cards are so easy to use and it's the easiest (and worse) type of debt you can accrue.

It's good to have them when really needed, but you have to learn how to use them wisely. The only reason you should ever use a credit card is convenience. Since you have an itemized list of everything you purchase through a credit card, you can better track your spending, plan a budget and have a better handle on record-keeping.

The trick is to religiously pay off the entire balance on the card every month. If you can't do that, then you should not buy the item.

One alternative to racking up credit card debt is to get rid of the temptation of the line of credit and use prepaid cards or debit cards for your purchases and to help you track purchases.

Most banks offer debit cards and you can get overdraft protection, which keeps you from racking up enormous fees if you go over the amount you have in your account. Prepaid cards are offered from most major credit card companies and involve you securing the money in the account, then paying it down and re-depositing when the balance is low.

You have to create and follow a budget if you want to avoid staying in debt forever. A budget is a detailed plan about how you're going to spend your money each month so that you can ensure that you won't go over a certain amount.

Also, budget some of your money after bills and necessities for savings or investing. There are a number of handy software packages which will help you track each dime you spend.

You should plan to fund an emergency reserve which totals about six months' worth of earnings. Then, make sure you withdraw money from the account only in case of an emergency or unforeseen medical expense.

There are also other means to get out of debt - including bankruptcy and credit or debt counseling services, but make sure you choose one that is non-profit rather than for-profit to learn how to resolve current debt and keep from getting back into debt in the future.

# Borrowing from Friends or Family

The general rule of thumb for borrowing from friends and family to reduce your debt is – don't. You're likely to get a much better deal from them than getting a loan from a bank or other lending institution, but the risk is personal and may mean inviting an eventual rift between the people involved.

One reason you should never borrow from family or friends is that it's so tempting to use the money for other purposes than paying off your debt. Going through a bank will ensure that you pay them and they will hound you if you don't.

There's also personal risk in getting a loan from someone you care about. The relationship could end up in shambles if you don't act responsibly to pay off the loan and use the money for other purchases so you're even deeper in debt than when you got the personal loan.

But if you run out of options and getting a loan from friends or family is your only way out, make sure you have a concrete plan for paying them back as soon as possible. That means creating a budget so you know you'll have the money when the time comes to pay it back.

A friend may balk at you paying interest on the loan, but you should insist. They could deposit the same amount of money in a bank and earn interest from it – so what you would be getting is actually them forfeiting income so they can help you out.

Insist on paying at least the rate of interest they might earn from a high-yield savings account. And if your friend offers less money than you need, don't keep asking for more. Graciously accept what they've offered and move on. Never negotiate a loan with a friend.

Document your loan. Create a payment plan on paper that outlines the amount and date each payment is due. Make sure you provide the lender with a copy so he knows when to expect your payment(s) and when the loan will be repaid in full.

After you both agree to the terms of the loan, stick to the plan. Never be late and don't come to your friend with excuses about why you're going to be late or can't pay the full amount. This is more than a business transaction – this is a personal relationship that could easily turn sour unless you stick to the plan.

If at all possible, pay off the loan early. Even if you think the friend or family member doesn't need the money right away, make every effort to improve your financial situation and to pay back the loan as soon as possible.

Make sure you pay it forward in your future dealings. The people who have helped you out of a financial jam may need the favor returned – or there may be someone else in your life that is going through much the same financial problems as you. Offer as much as you can to show your appreciation and your attitude and kindness.

# Credit Counseling Agencies – Do They Really Help?

Credit counseling or debt management services can help you get out of debt by providing you with a debt management plan to pay off your current debts. Never use a for-profit credit counseling agency.

Non-profit agencies are available that will not only help you get out of bad debts, but which will also help you consolidate your outstanding loans such as auto and student loans.

Your initial contact with a non-profit credit counseling agency will involve a meeting with a credit counselor. He or she will ask you for documentation about your consumer debt and have you fill out an application outlining your personal information.

If you're approved for the service, the agency you choose will then create a debt management plan that includes an account set up by the agency. You will deposit a certain amount of money each month which they will use to pay off your creditors.

There will be an interest fee, but it should be much lower than the APR on your debts. The service will then contact your debtors and negotiate a payment plan which will hopefully include a lower interest rate and lower payments.

After the payment plan is approved, the agency will begin to pay the debtors on an ongoing basis from the payment you will deposit each month.

Credit counseling services can also educate you about debt prevention in the future.

They'll also work with you after developing a debt relief plan and help you develop a workable budget and counsel you about investing and savings plans. Using a credit counseling service can actually improve your credit rather than hurt it.

You'll appear as determined to eliminating your debt and getting back on track with the help the credit counseling service provides. Your creditors may decide to re-age your account, meaning that they may forgive late fees incurred before you began the counseling process.

They may also agree not to report late or missed payments to credit bureaus. Non-profit credit counseling agencies can greatly help your decision to pay off and get out of debt. Just beware of credit counseling scams which promise variable-rate loans you can use to pay off debts – then, tack on high rate APRs or demand up-front fees for their services.

A checklist of requirements of reputable credit counseling agencies should include having a BBB (Better Business Bureau) membership, ensuring it's a non-profit agency and have accreditation and charge minimal fees for their services.

Customer references should be available from the agency you choose and they should also be willing to provide you with periodic reports about the status of your debts. Keep in mind that you, alone, are accountable for your debts, even if the service has agreed to pay them off.

**Consolidating Your Debts**

When you move to consolidate your outstanding debts, you'll be obtaining a new loan called a consolidation loan. You'll pay off the old debts with the new consolidation loan and then have one payment – usually at a lower APR and for a fixed term limit of three to five years.

The lender (a bank or credit union) will pay off your existing debts with the loan you secured and you'll now be responsible to pay off that loan and any other new debts you might incur in the meantime.

People usually opt for a consolidation loan when they would prefer a lower or fixed APR, pay only one bill rather than multiple or to pay one rate rather than rates that vary. Most types of debts can be consolidated, but people usually choose to consolidate personal loans or credit card debt.

You can choose from two types of consolidation loans – secured or unsecured. A secured loan is based on something you own that has value (an asset) and it should be worth enough to cover the consolidation loan.

An unsecured loan doesn't require assets to back the loan, making it risky for the lender and you might end up living with a higher APR, but if you don't have the collateral to offer, it's a good option.

The first step in getting a handle on consolidating your loans is to gather all of the information about your debts (recent copies of loan statements and other pertinent information) and list them in a way that shows the present balance and interest rates on each credit card.

You may choose to consolidate all your debts or only certain ones such as those with high interest rates, but most prefer to consolidate all of them at the same time. Determine the total amount of the debts you'll be consolidating and also figure the average APR on the loans by totaling the interest rates and then dividing it by the number of debts you're consolidating.

After consulting with lenders to decide if consolidation will help you and which loan is appropriate for your situation, apply for the loan. After you're approved for the loan, make sure you understand the terms. If your application is rejected, consider consulting with a credit counseling organization to formulate a get-out-of-debt plan.

If you get the consolidation loan, you'll either receive a check or the amount will be deposited into your checking account. Make sure you use that money to pay off the designated debts in full. Never use the loan to make another purchase.

The terms of your consolidation loan will determine your payment and how long it will take you to pay it off in full. Most loans will be paid back in the 3 to 5 years, but some can take as many as 20 or 30 years. Just make sure you get the type of loan that's best for your situation and that you can easily make the payments.

**Avoid Get Out of Debt Scams**

When you're desperate to get out of debt, you may be tempted to grab the first offer that comes along to relieve the pressure and chaos that debt can bring into your life. Unfortunately, there are get out of debt scams that can bring even more pressure and chaos into your life.

You should avoid them at all costs. These scammers target those with high credit card debt by claiming they will negotiate with the person's creditors or reduce payments or debt balance.

This is a false promise which can cost you an up-front fee and then fail to help you get out of debt or even lower payments or settle debt. If you have an auto loan that's in arrears, there are scams which claim they can reduce your monthly loan or lease payment to avoid repossession.

All of these scammers target those consumers who are in dire straits with their credit. Other scams want you to purchase their services which include removing information which impacts your negative credit reports with credit agencies, even if the report is truthful.

Even though the FTC (Federal Trade Commission) actively pursues those bogus credit services and bring lawsuits against them, there are numerous agencies out there that prey on those people desperate to get out of debt and misrepresent themselves as agencies which can help.

Payday loans are some of the worst scams claiming to help, but really make things worse by charging enormously high interest rates. Payday loans are actually short-term loans that prey on people in need who are desperate for quick money.

Other scammers use the Internet, telemarketing by phone and advertisements on radio programs to target their victims who are searching for debt relief. Some tempt people to enroll you in so-called financial hardship programs, claiming they'll negotiate with the creditors and promising the debt can be repaid in a short amount of time.

Some of these scams violate the FTC Act, which makes it unlawful to engage in deceptive practices. There is also a Telemarketing Sales Rule prohibiting deceptive telemarketing practices.

If you think you've been defrauded by a deceptive get out of debt scam, contact the FTC either online or by phone to find out how you can file a complaint. If you find you can't resolve your debt problems alone, seek out a legitimate agency such as the Consumer Credit Counseling Services.

It may take longer and be a bit more work on your part to get out of debt by doing it yourself, but you'll be able to better plot your future finances and how you'll handle spending at the end of the process.

# Steps to Financial Freedom

Realizing financial freedom means you can finally live the life you want. It's a tremendously freeing achievement that can help you feel secure, but it's elusive for most of us unless we take the proper steps to achieve it.

Paying yourself first is the first rule to achieving financial freedom. That means each pay day you should make it a habit to transfer part of your income (10 to 20 percent) to an investment account – and forget about it.

Another step to financial freedom is to pay down your credit card debt. This is considered consumer debt and is fraught with high interest rates and the inherent temptation to overspend.

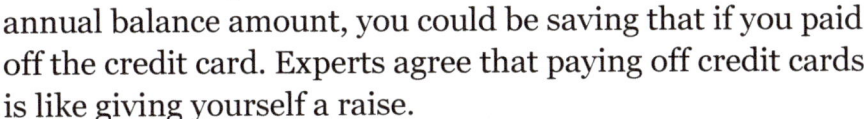

Even if you have a low interest rate on your annual balance amount, you could be saving that if you paid off the credit card. Experts agree that paying off credit cards is like giving yourself a raise.

Use tax advantage methods such as retirement savings, IRAs and MyRAs until you've maxed them out. Since most of us are uninformed about stocks and bonds, these methods are easy and proven ways to manage your investments.

If you can invest through your workplace, do it. Establish a monetary reserve to get you through tough times or unexpected expenses. Some recommend having a savings account with six to eight months' worth of net income while others claim that two months savings is enough.

Do what makes you feel most comfortable. Purchase a home only when you can easily afford it. A home can become a financial burden by requiring a higher payment, upkeep, insurance and other strains on the pocketbook.

Rather than making a small down payment, try for a larger down payment (such as 20% of the purchase price). Your mortgage is more likely to be approved by the lender and your home insurance will cost less.

It's best to purchase a lower priced home than one you're qualified to buy. The financial freedom of having enough money you need to feel secure both now and in the future is a tough goal to achieve in these tough times.

But, when you follow the advised steps to keep out of overwhelming debt and paying yourself first, you will eventually achieve the dream. You may have to adjust your lifestyle to live within your means – or below it.

Putting off taking an expensive vacation, choosing a less expensive place to live, foregoing private schools for the kids or paring down to one car gets you closer to financial freedom and the ability to achieve what you really want in life.

# Final Thoughts - Life After Debt

Understanding why you fell into the deep chasm of debt in the first place is the first step in resolving your issues with debt and building wealth for the future. Know that getting out from under the stigma of being in overwhelming debt can take years.

During the years of clawing your way out of the stigma of debt, it can be tempting to get back into debt with offers of credit cards and mismanaging your money – once again. Getting in debt again too soon can spiral you into another path of stress and debt that you're struggling to pay.

You should examine your relationship with debt and begin to analyze why you got into the predicament in the first place. You can begin to manage your debts effectively as you create a budget and follow it to the penny, diagnosing your spending habits along the way.

Credit cards are the main culprit of getting into more debt than you can handle. You can purchase more with credit cards without having to spend the money you have on hand. It feels like having free money.

So during your life after debt, you should only spend with money you have on hand. Purchasing all those good deals on a credit card means you're actually paying more money than the items originally cost because of the interest rates tacked onto the cost of your purchases for the privilege.

If you do use credit cards after you free yourself from overwhelming debt, make sure you pay them off in full each month to avoid excessive interest charges and to build good credit history.

Prepaid credit cards are good alternatives to other credit cards. You get a certain amount of credit according to the amount you put on it and make purchases that are deducted from that balance.

You can add more money to the card as you pay it down, making it work much like a phone card. Debit cards are also popular for those who want a documented account of their purchases and to help them from spending excessively again. Most banks offer debit cards issued by MasterCard or Visa.

You'll need to religiously track your spending if you hope to avoid getting back in debt and keep to a budget that is carefully planned. After you track spending for approximately a month, you'll have a pretty good idea about your expenses and where you can cut back.

Try to create a mindset for building wealth and making sure you've saved enough to meet unexpected expenses or loss of income. Besides saving money, research how you can invest your hard-earned dollars to make more money for you.

# Monthly Sample Budget

Here is a screenshot of a sample budget that tracks basic income and spending. You can adjust yours as necessary to reflect your actual specific income and spending categories.

| Category | Monthly Budget Amount | Actual Amount | Difference |
|---|---|---|---|
| **Monthly Sample Budget** | | | |
| **INCOME:** | | | |
| Wages/Income | $872 | $810 | $62 |
| Interest Income | $232 | $196 | $36 |
| ***INCOME SUBTOTAL*** | $1,104 | $1,006 | $98 |
| **EXPENSES:** | | | |
| Taxes | $386 | $397 | -$11 |
| Rent/Mortgage | $298 | $239 | $59 |
| Utilities | $99 | $95 | $4 |
| Groceries/Food | $121 | $100 | $21 |
| Clothing | $66 | $60 | $6 |
| Shopping | $55 | $46 | $9 |
| Entertainment | $44 | $44 | $0 |
| Miscellaneous/Other | $35 | $31 | $4 |
| ***EXPENSES SUBTOTAL*** | $1,104 | $1,012 | $92 |
| **NET INCOME (Income - Expenses)** | $0 | -$6 | |

# About the Author

I have published over 125 books on Amazon for Kindle, CreateSpace and other publishing platforms.

While most of my books are on health and fitness in general, as I age (now 65) at the time of this writing) my topics of interest are geared toward aging baby boomers and older.

Besides my own writing, I also ghostwrite ebooks, books, reports, articles, blogs and do Kindle conversions for clients on a variety of topics.

Today my wife and I are retired from our careers and live in Gold Canyon, AZ. I now write as a retirement business where you'll find me happily sitting in my office typing away on my laptop as I work on my next book or ghostwriting project . . . that is if we are not traveling on a cruise ship - our new-found mode of travel.

For a current list of published books, go to his Amazon Author Page at: https://www.amazon.com/-/e/B0072M6PYO

or his Createspace Page at:
https://www.createspace.com/pub/simplesitesearch.search.do?sitesearch_query=Ron+Kness&sitesearch_type=STORE

www.ingramcontent.com/pod-product-compliance
Lightning Source LLC
Chambersburg PA
CBHW041109180526
45172CB00001B/168